Polar Bears

Caroline Candusio

Polar bears live in cold, icy places.

What do polar bears do there?

Polar bears walk.

Their sharp claws are good for gripping the ice.

Polar bears **jump**.

Their strong legs are good for jumping.

Polar bears swim.

Their long bodies are good for swimming.

Polar bears **play**.

Their big paws are good for playing on slippery snow.

**Polar bears sleep.
They have had a busy day.**